YOU CHOOSE
BOOKS

SPIES OF THE
AMERICAN REVOLUTION

AN INTERACTIVE ESPIONAGE ADVENTURE

by Elizabeth Raum

Consultant:
Richard Bell, PhD
Associate Professor of History
University of Maryland, College Park

CAPSTONE PRESS
a capstone imprint

You Choose Books are published by Capstone Press,
1710 Roe Crest Drive, North Mankato, Minnesota 56003
www.capstonepub.com

Library of Congress Cataloging-in-Publication Data
Raum, Elizabeth.
Spies of the American Revolution : an interactive espionage adventure / by
Elizabeth Raum.
pages cm. — (You choose books. You choose: spies)
Includes bibliographical references and index.
Summary: "In You Choose format, explores the Revolutionary War from the perspectives of
spies on both the British and American sides"— Provided by publisher. Audience: Grade 4 to 6.
ISBN 978-1-4914-5858-7 (library binding)
ISBN 978-1-4914-5931-7 (paperback)
ISBN 978-1-4914-5943-0 (eBook PDF)
1. United States—History—Revolution, 1775–1783—Secret service—Juvenile literature. 2.
Espionage—History—18th century—Juvenile literature. 3. Spies—History—18th century—
Juvenile literature. I. Title.
E279.R38 2016
973.3'85—dc23   2015018523

Editorial Credits
Michelle Hasselius, editor; Ted Williams, art director; Rick Korab, designer;
Jo Miller, media researcher; Lori Barbeau, production specialist

Photo Credits
Alamy: Mary Evans Picture Library, 98; Bridgeman Images: Collection of the New York
Historical Society, USA, 31; Capstone Press: Terri Poburka, cover (silhouette), XNR
Productions, 8; Corbis, 25; Glow Images: Superstock, 6; Granger, NYC, 39, 47; iStockphoto:
Hulton Archive, 93; Landov: Ivy Close Images, 12, 81; Library of Congress, 21, 42, 50; Mary
Evans Picture Library: Richard Simkin, 62; Murals by Vance Locke courtesy of the Three
Village Central School District, 16, 19; National Archives and Records Administration, 35;
Newscom: akg-images, 75, Picture History, 41, 100, Prisma/Album, 64; North Wind Picture
Archives, 28, 36, 53, 57, 68, 72, 84, 86, 88, 95, Gary Embleton, 46, 85, Nancy Carter, 23;
Shutterstock: Lucy, cover (background)

Design Elements: Shutterstock: alexkar08

Printed in Canada   0315   8828FRF15

TABLE OF CONTENTS

ABOUT YOUR ADVENTURE

The Revolutionary War has erupted between Great Britain and Patriots in the American colonies. But the war is not only being fought with muskets and cannons on the battlefields. Spies on both sides are risking their lives to gather information that could affect who wins the war.

In this book you'll explore how the choices people made meant the difference between life and death. The events you'll experience happened to real people.

Chapter One sets the scene. Then you choose which path to read. Follow the directions at the bottom of each page. The choices you make will change your outcome. After you finish your path, go back and read the others for new perspectives and more adventures.

YOU CHOOSE the path you take through history.

6

American colonists in the 1700s

CHAPTER 1

THE WAR FOR INDEPENDENCE

In 1775 Great Britain rules the American colonies. Not everyone is happy about this. Many colonists feel that British laws are unfair, and British taxes are too high. The colonists who are against British rule call themselves Patriots. Those loyal to Great Britain are called Loyalists. Colonists dress alike, speak the same language, and live side by side. It's not always easy to tell who is a Patriot and who is a Loyalist.

7

TURN THE PAGE.

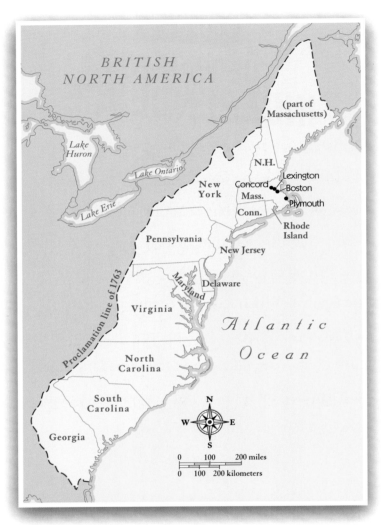

map of the 13 colonies that rebelled against Great Britain

In Boston, Massachusetts, Paul Revere organizes a group of craftsmen to spy on the British army. They call themselves the mechanics. They patrol the city after dark, keep track of British supplies and weapons, and warn of possible attacks on Patriot weapon storehouses. Paul Revere and his men are America's first spies.

Loyalists are spying too. British spies learn weapons are stored in Lexington and Concord, Massachusetts. The British army plans to march there. Patriot spies learn of the British plans and send Paul Revere to warn the other Patriots. On April 19, 1775, shots are fired in Lexington and Concord. The Revolutionary War has begun.

9

TURN THE PAGE.

Two months later, the Second Continental Congress makes George Washington commander in chief of the Continental army. The Continental army will fight against the British.

In September 1776 one of Washington's lieutenants, Nathan Hale, volunteers to spy on the British. He goes to Long Island, where the British army is in control. He doesn't blend in. He's a teacher by trade, not a spy. The British realize he's a spy. He's captured and hanged. General William Howe, commander of the British forces, ordered Hale's death. It's a warning—spies die. Hale is brave to the end and is said to have declared, "I only regret that I have but one life to lose for my country."

By 1777 General Henry Clinton has taken over as the British commander in chief of North America. He depends on a network of spies. Washington needs spies too. Spies are everywhere. They are brave, clever, and determined to help their side. Which spy are you?

11

TO SPY FOR THE PATRIOTS IN THE CULPER SPY RING, TURN TO PAGE 13.

TO SPY FOR THE BRITISH ARMY, TURN TO PAGE 43.

TO SEE WHAT LIFE WAS LIKE FOR A SLAVE SPYING IN THE WAR, TURN TO PAGE 73.

CHAPTER 2

GENERAL WASHINGTON'S SPY

It's late, and you're about to lock the tavern door. Your longtime friend and neighbor Abraham Woodhull stops in. "Abraham, welcome!" you say.

Abraham is a farmer, and these days farming is good work. The British army has occupied Long Island for nearly two years. Farmers have plenty of people buying their produce.

13

Abraham seems relieved that the tavern is empty. "We need to talk," he whispers.

His news is stunning. Abraham Woodhull is a spy! He's George Washington's spy, and he wants you to join him.

TURN THE PAGE.

"I've always favored independence," you say. "I'll do what I can."

Abraham tells you that Washington needs information—good intelligence. He wants to know what the British army will do next.

You meet the next night in Abraham's barn. Caleb Brewster is there too. You grew up with Brewster in Setauket, Long Island. He is the captain of a small whaleboat.

Abraham explains the plan. He'll go into Manhattan, New York, and spend time with his sister. She runs a boardinghouse there.

"There's nothing suspicious about a man visiting his sister," Abraham says. "I'll learn what I can about British plans in New York." Abraham turns to you. "You'll come to the city and pick up my information. You can claim to be buying supplies for the tavern," he suggests.

"Give the information to Caleb. He'll sail across Long Island Sound to Connecticut. Benjamin Tallmadge will get it to General Washington," Abraham says.

Tallmadge, another friend from Setauket, is a major in the Continental army. "Washington has put Benjamin in charge of his spies. Benjamin has promised never to reveal our names, not even to George Washington," Abraham says. "We'll use codes. My code name is Culper, Samuel Culper. Our very lives depend on keeping secrets."

Abraham leaves the next day for Manhattan. You wait two weeks before going to the city. It's a 55-mile trip. The first few times you go, everything works perfectly. You go to the city and pick up Abraham's reports on the location and number of British troops in the city.

TURN THE PAGE.

When you get home, you add notes of your own before giving the papers to Brewster. He adds details about British navy ships. Then he rows across Long Island Sound to Connecticut, which is still in Patriot hands. Tallmadge passes the intelligence to Washington.

One day in January, you start another journey to New York. You're almost there, when you notice a British army patrol ahead. Should you keep going?

Abraham Woodhull (left) and Caleb Brewster (right) transported messages to Washington.

16

TO CONTINUE ON, GO TO PAGE 17.

TO TURN BACK, TURN TO PAGE 18.

There's nothing to fear. British army patrols are common. You answer their questions and move on.

When you arrive in the city, you find Abraham in a state of panic. "George Washington is pleased with our information. He wants to meet me," Abraham says nervously. "I said no. It's too dangerous."

"We're all being careful," you assure him. "No one will find out who we are."

"Maybe not," he says. "But I must return to Setauket. I fear the British army is following me."

You bring the reports to Brewster. The spy business is taking its toll on your tavern business. If you neglect the tavern, will the British army become suspicious? Should you get someone else to carry the messages?

TO RECRUIT A MESSENGER, TURN TO PAGE 20.

TO CONTINUE GOING TO NEW YORK, TURN TO PAGE 22.

There's no point in inviting trouble. You try to avoid the British army whenever you can. But on Long Island, that's nearly impossible. You turn into the woods to give the soldiers time to pass.

As soon as you return to the road three horsemen gallop out of the woods, firing their rifles. Robbers!

You urge your horse forward at a full gallop. A shot whizzes past your head. Another rips through your jacket, but your horse races on. Twenty minutes later, the sound of horses behind you has faded. You're safe. You take a deep breath. Something's wrong. You feel dizzy, and your arm throbs. You make it home and collapse at the tavern door.

The musket ball that ripped your jacket is lodged in your arm. When British soldiers ask what happened, you answer truthfully. "Robbers," you say.

You'll heal, but you won't be making trips to New York for a while. But Abraham is depending on you.

Austin Roe carried messages for the Culper Spy Ring.

TO RECRUIT A MESSENGER TO TAKE OVER, **TURN TO PAGE 20.**

TO TALK TO CALEB BREWSTER, **TURN TO PAGE 25.**

19

You ask Jonas Hawkins to carry messages from New York. You trust him. But you tell him as little as possible. Secrecy is vital.

Abraham is upset. He doesn't trust Hawkins. "He's too nervous," Abraham says.

Hawkins proves him right. When Hawkins fears the British army has labeled him a spy, he destroys Abraham's reports for Washington.

"I risked my life collecting that information," Abraham rages.

"At least he wasn't caught," you say. But from

20 now on, you'll do the work yourself.

The long trip to the city is dangerous. You slog through snow and submit to British army searches. Robbers try to steal what little gold you carry.

By April 1779, the spy ring has created a codebook. Numbers replace names. Number 727 stands for New York. Abraham is number 722. Brewster is number 725. General Washington is number 711. Even if the British army finds a message, they won't be able to read it.

On your next trip to New York, Abraham asks you to go with him to a coffeehouse. But it's been a long journey.

a page from the Culper Spy Book

TO INSIST ON LEAVING, TURN TO PAGE 27.

TO GO TO THE COFFEEHOUSE, TURN TO PAGE 31.

It's safer to hire someone to help at the tavern. You won't have to reveal any secrets. You go to New York about every two weeks, but you're careful not to follow a pattern. That might alert the British army.

Abraham and Tallmadge make a codebook. Important names, places, and words are given numbers. Abraham hands you a message.

"Every 356 is opened at the entrance of 727, and every 371 is searched. In the future every 356 must be 691 with the 286 received," you read out loud. "What does it mean?"

"Every *letter* is opened at the entrance of *New York*, and every *man* is searched. In the future every *letter* must be *written* with the *ink* received," Abraham says.

"What ink?" you ask.

"Invisible ink. We must use the whitest paper," Abraham says. "Invisible ink is white. It disappears on the page until the person receiving it dabs a reagent, or special liquid, on the letter. General Washington left orders to fold the paper in a certain way, so he'll know it has a hidden message. It's safer than just using the code. We will use both."

Colonists dipped quill pens in ink to write letters.

TURN THE PAGE.

You carry the messages with invisible ink for several months. But you sense a growing danger.

"The British are suspicious," Abraham says. "I am returning to Setauket. Robert Townsend will take my place." Townsend is a merchant. He also writes for a Loyalist newspaper. "No one will guess he's a Patriot spy," Abraham says. "British officers talk freely about their plans around him."

Townsend's intelligence is even better than Abraham's. But these are dangerous times. Everyone leaving the city is searched. Sooner or later, someone will realize that the blank papers you carry contain secret messages.

24

"It might be better if Townsend meets you at a safe house on Long Island," Abraham tells you. "But we cannot risk Townsend being discovered."

TO MEET TOWNSEND AT A SAFE HOUSE, TURN TO PAGE 34.

TO GO TO THE CITY, TURN TO PAGE 38.

Where is Brewster? He hides his whaleboat in one of the many coves on Long Island Sound. But which one?

Abraham and another spy, Anna Strong, have worked out a code. A black coat on her clothesline means Brewster is here. The number of handkerchiefs on the line tells which cove he is waiting in. There's a black coat and five handkerchiefs on the clothesline. You make your way to his hiding place. But the cove is empty.

view of New York from Long Island in 1776

TO RETURN TO THE TAVERN, TURN TO PAGE 26.

TO WAIT FOR BREWSTER, TURN TO PAGE 30.

Perhaps you misunderstood the clothesline code. Is it a sign that you should continue as messenger? Luckily your arm heals quickly. A local bookseller mentions he is making a trip to Manhattan.

"I must go too," you say. "It will be safer if we travel together."

Once you reach the city, he goes off to a bookstore. You meet Abraham at his sister's boardinghouse.

26

TURN TO PAGE 31.

You tell Abraham you can't go. "Then at least come to my room," Abraham says. "There's something I must show you." He hands you a white sheet of paper.

"It's empty," you say.

"You're wrong, my friend. I've written a full report in invisible ink," Abraham says. "Washington has a special liquid called a reagent that will make the letters reappear."

He hands you a written letter to his father. On a second blank page, he scrawls some words. "No one will know that a secret message is hidden there," he says.

27

You put the pages in your pack and go to the ferry. When you get there, a British army patrol stops you and demands to look in your pack.

TO LET HIM LOOK, TURN TO PAGE 28.

TO PROTEST, TURN TO PAGE 36.

You remain calm and hand over your pack.
There's not much inside—a piece of cloth for
your wife, some rolls to eat on the journey,
and the letter to Abraham's father. The British
soldier looks at the letter, reads it, and stuffs it
back inside.

"Go," he says.

British army patrols looked for spies among the colonists.

For the next several months, you bring messages from Manhattan to Long Island. The next summer, Abraham returns to Setauket. He has a new spy in New York. Robert Townsend has access to British officers and their secrets.

British soldiers are everywhere. Everyone is getting nervous the spy ring will be discovered. Everyone except for Brewster. He braves the water on the stormy days and sneaks past British army patrols. What courage!

"Do you want to come along?" he asks. "If so, meet me at dusk by West Meadow."

You're there on time. But Brewster is not. Perhaps you should check the next cove.

TO WAIT AT WEST MEADOW, TURN TO PAGE 30.

TO CHECK THE NEXT COVE, TURN TO PAGE 40.

Brewster will come soon. You sit beneath a tree and fall asleep.

"Get up!" someone roars. The point of a bayonet nudges your chin. "You're under arrest."

British soldiers question you for hours. Luckily you have no papers on you. Nothing can identify you as a spy.

"Why were you at the cove?" the soldier asks.

"I like the sea air. Can't a man enjoy a walk on the beach?" you protest. "You know me. You drink at my tavern. I have nothing to do with this war."

30

Eventually they let you go. "We'll be watching you," the soldier says.

Your days as a spy are over. The British army is watching, and you can't put others in danger.

TURN TO PAGE 41.

"There's someone you must meet," Abraham insists.

You go with Abraham to James Rivington's new coffeehouse. Rivington also owns a print shop. He appears loyal to Great Britain, but he's really a Patriot. You and Abraham can talk freely in the noisy coffeehouse.

James Rivington

TURN THE PAGE.

Abraham introduces you to Robert Townsend, who was born and raised in Oyster Bay, Long Island. Townsend owns a small store in Manhattan. British soldiers and their wives often shop there. He also writes a column for Rivington's newspaper, *The Royal Gazette*. The soldiers like to see their names in print. Everyone assumes that Townsend is a Loyalist. But that's not the real story.

"Townsend is one of us," Abraham says. "I'm no longer safe in New York. From now on, you'll get your reports from Townsend. His code name is Culper, Jr. I am now Culper, Sr."

You carry Robert Townsend's reports. He discovers a British plan to print fake money. He also finds out about an attack on French forces landing in Rhode Island to help the Patriots.

General Washington stops both plans thanks to his spies.

You worry the British army is growing suspicious. The danger increases each day. Townsend wants to quit. So does Abraham. Brewster is as brave as ever, but he is being watched. So are you.

"I'll carry the reports one more time," you offer.

"Townsend is willing to come to a safe house on Long Island," Abraham tells you. "Or you can go into the city again."

33

TO MEET AT A SAFE HOUSE, **TURN TO PAGE 34.**

TO GO TO THE CITY, **TURN TO PAGE 38.**

You agree to meet at the home of a Patriot on Long Island. He welcomes you. His wife offers you coffee while you wait for Robert Townsend. But Townsend doesn't come.

You return the next day. There is still no sign of Townsend. Has something happened?

Two weeks later, Townsend arrives in Setauket. He never explains what happened, but he is frightened. "I cannot return to the city," he says. "It's too dangerous." The spy ring shuts down. It's a welcome break.

In the summer of 1780, Tallmadge asks everyone to resume spying. It's what General Washington wants. You all agree.

The spy ring then uncovers some startling news. The Patriot General Benedict Arnold has switched sides—he's working with the British army. Arnold avoids capture and is now a powerful enemy. The Culper Spy Ring goes into hiding until the war ends.

Benedict Arnold

TURN TO PAGE 41.

"There's just a few personal items in the pack, sir," you say, gripping it tightly.

"We'll see about that," the soldier says, as he rips the pack out of your hands. He tears open a piece of fabric you've purchased for your wife and tosses it into the mud. He pulls out the rolls you bought for lunch. He hands one to his friend and takes a big bite out of the other.

American colonists were often forced to share their food, supplies, and even their homes with British soldiers.

"Please, sir. You have no business … " you say.

"No business?" the soldier says. "Whatever you do is our business." He pulls the letter out of your pack, scans it, and tears it to pieces. At least no one will discover its secrets.

But you've had enough. "Give me my things or I'll … " you shout.

The soldier slams the butt of his musket into your chest. You stumble and fall to the ground, hitting your head on a large rock. You die instantly. Pieces of the torn message dance in the breeze.

37

THE
-END-

To follow another path, turn to page 11.
To read the conclusion, turn to page 101.

You agree to take one more trip to New York. After all it will be safer for Townsend if you go to him.

Townsend gives you some messages written in invisible ink. You have no idea what the blank pages say. You only know that it's important to get them to General Washington.

You're searched at the ferry. Everyone is. But this time, you cannot talk your way through. The British soldier notices the blank pages and calls for an officer.

"We were told to watch for this sort of thing," he says.

British soldiers question you for hours. You say nothing. They transfer you to the prison ship, the HMS *Jersey*. Conditions are terrible. Those who don't die of disease starve to death.

You manage to survive. But when you return home, you are half-starved and very ill. You die a few months later of an unknown fever.

About 11,000 prisoners died on British prison ships like the HMS Jersey *during the course of the war.*

THE
-END-

To follow another path, turn to page 11.
To read the conclusion, turn to page 101.

Brewster's boat is hidden in the next cove. "A British army patrol boat was heading for West Meadow," Brewster says. "Climb aboard."

The water is choppy. The small boat bounces on the waves. In Connecticut Brewster delivers secrets to a rider who will take them to Washington in New Jersey.

"This is our way of winning the war," Brewster says. "No one may know our names. But we're doing our part to win independence, just as surely as the soldiers on the battlefield."

Brewster's words give you new energy to continue being Washington's spy. You remain in the Culper Spy Ring until the end of the war.

THE
-END-

To follow another path, turn to page 11.
To read the conclusion, turn to page 101.

You keep quiet until the United States Constitution is ratified in 1789. When customers stop by to celebrate the new Constitution, you proudly say, "I was General Washington's spy."

You never reveal the names of the other members of the Culper Spy Ring, but you enjoy recounting your own adventures as a spy.

one of the first newspaper printings of the U.S. Constitution in 1787

THE -END-

To follow another path, turn to page 11.
To read the conclusion, turn to page 101.

Philadelphia waterfront in the 1770s

CHAPTER 3

GENERAL CLINTON'S SPY

Life is good in America's biggest city, Philadelphia, Pennsylvania. Yes, you pay taxes to the British. But in return, they protect the colonies and encourage trade. Your books come from England. So do your dresses and other goods. Some colonists want independence from Great Britain, but you remain loyal.

TURN THE PAGE.

In September 1777, British General William Howe and his troops occupy the city.

Soon after the troops arrive you meet Joseph Bates, a British soldier. Eventually you and Joseph marry.

Joseph is an expert on guns and cannons. He enjoys talking about weapons. One day when his friends stop by, you point to a cannon and say, "Isn't that a howitzer? It fires six-pound explosive shells."

"Yes," Joseph says with pride.

44   One of Joseph's friends is Mr. Cregge, who works for British General Clinton. "He gathers intelligence," Joseph says.

"He's a spy?" you ask.

"Shh, I'm not supposed to know," Joseph cautions. "It's our secret."

One day Joseph tells you that he's leaving. "General Clinton is taking us north. The Patriots will move into Philadelphia," he says. "It will be a quiet takeover, no fighting." But you are uneasy.

When Mr. Cregge stops by, he takes you aside. "The British army can use a woman like you," Mr. Cregge says. "No one would suspect a woman of spying."

You gasp. "You want me to spy for the British army?"

"Yes," he says. "Your knowledge of weapons will serve you well."

45

"But I've never shot a musket," you say.

"You won't need to," he says. "Your work will not be on the battlefield. Get to Clinton's New York headquarters as quickly as possible. Tell his aide I sent you. Tell no one—not even Joseph."

TURN THE PAGE.

You agree to become a spy. It will be good to help the British.

Joseph's regiment will leave for New York on June 18, 1778. Maybe you should follow the troops. Many women do. They are called camp followers. However you might get there faster on your own, if you're willing to risk the dangers a woman faces when traveling alone.

Camp followers were soldiers' wives who traveled with the troops. They sewed and cooked for the men.

46

TO GO TO NEW YORK ALONE, GO TO PAGE 47.

TO FOLLOW THE TROOPS, TURN TO PAGE 49.

You bring a change of clothing, a needle and thread, soap, and candles in a small pack. The Patriots are in charge of the city, and no one can leave without a pass. You go to the Patriot headquarters at the Masters-Penn House.

"My mother is ill in New York," you lie. "I must go to her. I need a pass."

The sentry gives you a pass signed by Benedict Arnold, the general in charge.

The Masters-Penn House was later home to George Washington and John Adams during their presidencies.

TURN THE PAGE.

You'll take a boat as far as Bordentown, New Jersey. You pay the fare out of your small savings.

At Bordentown the boat captain warns, "The roads are dangerous. It's not just robbers. Soldiers are tense. They may shoot before they ask questions."

It will take several days to walk to New York. You take cover behind trees and hedges on the side of the road whenever anyone comes by. One day you hear a wagon rumbling behind you. It looks like a farm wagon, but you won't know until it gets closer.

48

TO STAY HIDDEN, TURN TO PAGE 50.

TO WAIT FOR THE WAGON, TURN TO PAGE 53.

You join the women who follow the troops. Most are soldiers' wives. Others earn money washing and cooking for the troops. It's a slow march across New Jersey. More than 14,000 soldiers, supply wagons, and camp followers make up a company that stretches across 16 miles of countryside. About a week after you leave Philadelphia, you reach Bordentown, New Jersey.

"There's been a change of plans," Joseph says. "General Clinton is taking us east to the coast. The Patriot General Horatio Gates is marching south to block our way."

You don't want to get caught in a battle. Maybe you should leave and go to New York on your own.

49

TO GO NORTH ALONE, TURN TO PAGE 53.

TO STAY WITH THE TROOPS, TURN TO PAGE 56.

You stay hidden. It's safer not to take chances. In late July, you reach New York and report to the British army headquarters.

"Mr. Cregge sent me," you say to General Clinton's aide.

The aide ushers you inside. "General Clinton wants to know everything possible about George Washington's Continental army," he says. "How many men does he have? What weapons?"

"How can I help?" you ask.

Soldiers on both sides used weapons such as muskets, bayonets, cannons, and swords.

"Go to White Plains, New York, where the Continental army is stationed," the aide says. "Find a soldier named Chambers. He has been collecting information we need. Get it from him, and bring it to me."

The aide gives you a tiny piece of green silk. "It's called a token," he says. "It will identify you as a British agent. Use it only if you must." You push it deep into your pocket. "Good luck, Mrs. Barnes," he says.

"But my name is not Barnes. It's ... " you say.

General Clinton's aide puts a finger to his lips. "From now on, you are Mrs. Barnes. Never reveal your real name," he warns.

51

He gives you some money. You can buy supplies and pose as a peddler. Or you can save it to use later.

TO SAVE THE MONEY, TURN TO PAGE 52.

TO BUY SUPPLIES, TURN TO PAGE 58.

You pocket the money and begin your journey. You spend the night at a house owned by Loyalists. You reach General Washington's camp the next day.

You tell the sentry that you are looking for Chambers. "He is my cousin," you say. "His wife is ill."

You wander around the camp asking for Chambers. No one seems to know him. You count soldiers, weapons, and supplies as you walk. You count the cannons behind the Purdy house, where General Washington is staying. You remember what you see. It's too dangerous to write it down.

52

On August 2 you leave White Plains. You haven't gone far when you see a man by the road. He calls out to you. Is he hurt?

TO GO TO HIM, TURN TO PAGE 59.

TO FLEE, TURN TO PAGE 69.

A friendly farmer offers you a ride in his wagon full of cabbages, broccoli, and asparagus. "I'll sell them to the British army in New York," he says.

You reach the city on June 30. The farmer drops you and his vegetables off at the British army headquarters.

Colonists walked or used horses, wagons, boats, or stagecoaches to travel long distances.

53

TURN THE PAGE.

You speak with the officer in charge.
He takes you to General Clinton's top aide.

"Mr. Cregge sent you?" the aide asks.
"Excellent." He explains the dangers that a spy
faces. "If you are caught, you could be hanged.
At the very least, you'll be jailed," he warns.
"The roads are dangerous these days, for anyone.
Be careful. Robbers attack travelers. It doesn't
matter what side you're on."

"I'll use care," you say.

He gives you a small piece of green fabric.
"This is called a token," he says. "It will prove
that you are working for us. Guard it well."

The aide sends you on your first mission.
"The Continental commander, General George
Washington, is camped in northern New Jersey,"
he says. "Go there and see what you can learn."

You find Washington's camp and show the sentry the pass signed by General Arnold.

"I'm looking for my husband," you lie. The sentry signals you into the camp.

You roam through the camp. No one stops you. You notice everything—16,000 men, 30 field guns, and 700 wagons loaded with supplies. You don't write anything down—it's too dangerous. You keep it all in your head.

Five days later, you leave the Patriot camp. Night falls as you reach a small village. You're eager to get the information to General Clinton, but it's late. The Red Bull tavern is on one side of Main Street. A bookstore is on the other. The tavern serves supper, but the bookstore looks more cheerful. A woman stands at the counter.

55

TO GO TO THE RED BULL TAVERN, TURN TO PAGE 61.

TO GO TO THE BOOKSTORE, TURN TO PAGE 63.

It is dangerous for a woman to travel alone. You stay with the troops. But you tell Joseph not to worry if you leave suddenly.

"I may return home with some of the women," you say, "and I may not have a chance to tell you." He understands.

You cook and wash clothes for Joseph. One night you go for a walk and notice a spark of light in a nearby grove of trees. What is it? You see a man lighting his pipe. Another joins him. Something isn't right. You sneak closer, using the trees as cover.

56

"Washington has ordered the Patriot militias to attack British army camps," one man says. "You're to inform Captain John Outwater of the Bergen County Regiment."

The men are Patriot spies! You move a bit closer to get a good look. *Snap!* You step on a twig. The men run toward you.

It was often safer for spies to gather information at night.

TO RUN TO CAMP, TURN TO PAGE 64.

TO RUN INTO THE WOODS, TURN TO PAGE 65.

Peddlers are welcome in army camps. You buy thread, needles, and combs. You pack them into a bandana. You put the tiny piece of green fabric there too for safekeeping. You tie the bundle on a stick and carry it over your shoulder.

You walk much of the 30 miles to White Plains. A mile or two from Washington's camp, you pass a farmhouse. Laundry flaps in the breeze. It might be easier to enter the camp disguised as a man.

58

TO STEAL THE CLOTHES, TURN TO PAGE 66.

TO PASS BY THE FARMHOUSE, TURN TO PAGE 68.

You go to help him. As you get close, he yells, "She's a spy!" Two men in Continental army uniforms rush forward.

At first you deny it. "I'm not a spy," you say. "I was looking for my husband."

The man speaks up. "You told me you were looking for your cousin."

Had you said your cousin? Or had you said your husband? You pause, and that makes you look guilty.

The men take you to one of Washington's aides. "Put her under guard," the aide says. "And remember General Washington's orders. Treat her well. He said our prisoners must have no reason to complain."

TURN THE PAGE.

The Patriot soldiers are kind. One brings you a candle and a clean blanket. But no one can help you when you fall ill.

The camp doctor visits. "It's smallpox," he says. "It's spreading through the camp."

Some recover. You don't. You die in the Patriot camp, far from your beloved Philadelphia and Joseph.

THE
-END-

To follow another path, turn to page 11.
To read the conclusion, turn to page 101.

You're hungry. You enter the Red Bull tavern. The first man you see is wearing the blue uniform of George Washington's Continental army. This is a Patriot tavern, and you've interrupted some sort of meeting. You turn to leave. But several men get up to block your way.

"Is there a problem?" one man asks.

"No problem," you say, but your heart is pounding and your breath quickens. "I'm looking for my husband," you lie and peer into the crowd. "But he's not here. Sorry to have troubled you."

The men move aside, but you fear they don't believe you. As soon as you step outside, you run into the woods nearby. You rest behind a tree and listen to make sure no one has followed you.

61

TURN THE PAGE.

You trudge through the woods all night.
As the sun rises, you hear the tramp of soldiers.
You see their red coats. It's the British army!
They help you reach General Clinton. He offers
you another mission, but you refuse.

You stay with Joseph and his unit throughout
the war. When the British surrender in
Yorktown, Virginia, you sail to England. You
never tell Joseph about your ill-fated attempt
to spy for the British army.

*The British
army wore
red uniforms.
They were
often called
Redcoats.*

THE
-END-

To follow another path, turn to page 11.
To read the conclusion, turn to page 101.

The woman at the bookstore is kind. She offers you tea. It's a good sign. Only Loyalists serve tea—the Patriots forbid it.

"I am looking for a safe place to stay," you say. You lay the green cloth on the table. If she doesn't recognize it, you will pretend it's a handkerchief.

The woman nods. "Come with me," she says. She takes you home and introduces you to her husband. They explain the system of safe houses that dot New Jersey. "These people will help you," she says.

The next morning you thank them for their kindness. As you begin the trip back to General Clinton's New York headquarters, you hear a cannon and the blast of muskets in the distance. You hurry on. You'll fight this war with information, not bullets.

63

TURN TO PAGE 70.

You run toward the British army camp. The campfires grow brighter as you get closer. Feet pound behind you. You run right into the arms of a sentry. "Patriots," you gasp. "There!"

"Go tell the captain what you saw," he says. "Patriots!" he yells, and several men rush to help.

You go to General Clinton's tent and tell him the story. "Mr. Cregge said you need information," you say.

"He's right," General Clinton says. "You've already helped."

64

British General Henry Clinton

TURN TO PAGE 70.

You run into the woods and crash through the underbrush. You sink down beside a tree.

Eventually you get up and walk into a clearing. Men are sitting around a campfire.

"Joseph!" you call, rushing forward.

By the time you realize you're back at the Patriot camp, it's too late. This time there's no escape. The men tie you to a tree. You struggle, but the ropes are too tight. The men leave the next morning.

"Help me!" you cry. You regret telling Joseph not to worry if you disappear. No one comes to help. You grow weaker by the day, until you die tied to a tree in the New Jersey woods.

65

THE
-END-

To follow another path, turn to page 11.
To read the conclusion, turn to page 101.

You pull the clothes off the line.

"Stop! Thief!"

You turn and trip over a tree root. A man looms over you. His wife picks up your peddler's pack, opens it, and sorts through your items. She holds out the tiny green cloth.

The man nods. His shoulders relax, and he smiles. "A token," he says. "You're one of us!"

Relief floods through you. They're Loyalists! The token changes everything. You explain that you wanted to disguise yourself as a man to enter

General Washington's camp.

"You're safer as a woman," the man says. "No one notices women."

And no one questions your right to be at the Patriot camp. You go from tent to tent, selling small items to soldiers.

You go to Washington's headquarters and offer goods to the officers there. A captain who just arrived from Connecticut asks about a future attack. The others start to discuss Washington's plans. You listen carefully. One officer looks at you and signals to the others.

"Don't worry. She's just a peddler," one scoffs.

But when an unknown officer enters the room, the conversation ends. You slip away. You return to New York full of secrets for the British army.

67

TURN TO PAGE 70.

You pass the farmhouse. Being a woman may work to your advantage.

At the Patriot camp, a sentry motions you in. You peddle your items for several days, counting men and weapons as you walk. You note the weight of the cannonballs, the condition of the soldiers' uniforms, and the kinds of supplies and food available. Before dawn one morning, you sneak out of camp to report back to New York.

soldiers at a Continental army camp

TURN TO PAGE 71.

You flee in the opposite direction. Dangerous men called Cowboys and Skinners attack travelers. Cowboys are pro-British bandits. Skinners side with the Patriots. They are equally dangerous. You must be careful. General Clinton is waiting for your report.

69

TURN TO PAGE 71.

You work as a spy for the British army for two years. You move in and out of Patriot camps, counting artillery, men, and supplies. You listen for secrets and carry them back to the British army. No one ever notices you, and that explains your success.

After the war, you and Joseph move to Canada. Many Loyalists settle there. You become a teacher. You make many friends. Finally at age 80, you write an account of your secret life as a British army spy.

THE
-END-

To follow another path, turn to page 11.
To read the conclusion, turn to page 101.

When you return to New York, General Clinton is pleased. You've done so well, he sends you on another mission. You spend two years spying for General Clinton. Sometimes you are caught, but you always manage to convince the Patriots of your innocence. They never realize that you are General Clinton's secret weapon.

After several more spy missions, you ask permission to join Joseph in Virginia. In 1781 as the war winds down, you and Joseph travel to England. It will be your home now. You live a quiet life, never revealing your past as a British army spy.

THE
-END-

To follow another path, turn to page 11.
To read the conclusion, turn to page 101.

Many plantation owners in Virginia had slaves in the 1700s.

CHAPTER 4
THE SLAVE SPY

Mr. Armistead's slaves gather each night behind their living quarters. You're a house slave, but you sneak out to join them. You share the news of Patrick Henry's speech before the legislature in Virginia. "Give me liberty or give me death!" you quote.

Slaves want liberty too. Lord Dunmore, the British governor of Virginia, has promised freedom to any slave who helps the British army. Some are prepared to do so.

Your master, William Armistead of Virginia, is a Patriot. He wants freedom from England. Freedom for white Americans, that is. Not freedom for his slaves.

TURN THE PAGE.

One morning in the spring of 1777, you learn that 15 slaves are missing—12 men, one woman, and two young boys. Your master shakes his head.

"They've gone to join the British army. I was afraid of this." He looks at you. "Will you join them too?"

"No, sir," you say. Mr. Armistead taught you to read, write, and do math. You act as his secretary and keep his accounts. You live fairly well. You want to be free, but running away is dangerous. Owners punish runaways harshly.

At first most of the Revolutionary War battles take place in the north. But in 1779 the British army moves south. They capture South Carolina. It is only a matter of time until the fighting reaches Virginia.

In 1781 Mr. Armistead takes charge of the commissary, a store where soldiers buy their supplies. You go along as his clerk.

One day the Marquis de Lafayette walks into the store. He is a dashing 23-year-old general from France. He wears a navy blue Continental army uniform with gold trim and gold braiding.

"General Washington has his spies in New York," Lafayette says to Mr. Armistead. "We need spies here in Virginia too."

The Marquis de Lafayette

TURN THE PAGE.

Later you approach Mr. Armistead. "I could be a spy," you say.

"A slave as a spy?" he asks.

"Who would suspect a slave?" you say.

Mr. Armistead smiles. "And what would you expect in return?"

"Freedom," you say.

"Agreed," he says. You hope he means your freedom, not just America's.

General Lafayette is pleased. He hands you a letter written in code. "Deliver this to Lieutenant Colonel Jeremiah Olney of the First Rhode Island Regiment," he says. "They're camped a day's journey from here. Wait for his response and then hurry back."

You wear a field worker's simple cotton shirt and trousers. You tuck the folded message under the rope that serves as your belt.

"Walk along the roadway," General Lafayette says. "Don't rush. Remember you are a farm worker. Running will make you look suspicious. British soldiers are everywhere."

It's early morning when you leave Richmond. You walk down the dirt road. *Thump! Thump!* It takes a second to recognize the sound of British soldiers marching along the road. You slip behind a hedge and wait until they pass.

The sound dies away, and you step back onto the road. Suddenly three more British soldiers ride up on horseback.

77

TO STAY WHERE YOU ARE, TURN TO PAGE 78.

TO RUN BACK TO THE HEDGE, TURN TO PAGE 79.

Your orders were not to rush, so you stay put. You hang your head as the soldiers pass. They ignore you. As soon as they are out of sight, you continue on to the First Rhode Island Regiment's camp.

A sentry takes you directly to Colonel Olney. He hands the message to an aide, who deciphers it and hands it back to the colonel. Colonel Olney tells the aide to give you supper while he writes his reply.

78

When you return, a white man wearing a militia uniform waits nearby. "I need two men," Colonel Olney says. "We must send this original message on to General Washington and send a reply to Lafayette."

TO GO TO GENERAL WASHINGTON, TURN TO PAGE 82.

TO RETURN TO LAFAYETTE, TURN TO PAGE 83.

Their bayonets glint in the sun. Fear takes over. You run toward the shrubs, but it's too late. The British officers have seen you. A lieutenant leaps off his horse, tackles you, and drags you back to the road. Your rope belt comes loose, and Lafayette's message falls to the ground.

TO IGNORE THE MESSAGE, TURN TO PAGE 80.

TO REACH FOR THE MESSAGE, TURN TO PAGE 86.

You ignore the message. The officers don't seem to notice it. The captain in charge barks, "Who are you, and what are you doing?"

You hang your head and fold your hands. "My master told me to check the crops," you say. "He'll be angry if I don't come home soon."

"Where are you from?" the captain asks. You point to a house in the distance.

"That's Arnold Smythe's place. He's a Loyalist. Go home to your master," he says to you. He looks at his soldiers. "There's nothing gained in upsetting Britain's loyal subjects."

The men let you go and ride away. It was a close call. You retrieve the fallen message and continue on. You won't be caught a second time.

Despite your run-in with the British soldiers, you reach the Rhode Island camp before nightfall.

It doesn't take long to locate Colonel Olney's headquarters. The colonel sits at a rough desk in his tent and deciphers the message.

"You did well," he says and signals for his aide. The aide returns with a man in a Continental army uniform. "Gabney carries messages for me. One of you must take this message to Washington. Another will carry my reply to Lafayette."

the First Rhode
Island Regiment

81

TO GO TO GENERAL WASHINGTON, TURN TO PAGE 82.

TO RETURN TO GENERAL LAFAYETTE, TURN TO PAGE 83.

"You won't have to go far," the colonel's aide says. "It's only a day's journey."

"Is General Washington nearby?" you ask.

"No, but you're only going as far as Alexandria, Virginia," he says. "Others will carry the message to General Washington."

The aide gives you instructions about the drop. "Wait until dark. Then go to the large brick church with a graveyard beside it. Find the grave of Atticus Whitney," he says. "Place the message beneath the pot of red flowers. It's a dead drop. This means you leave the message, and another agent will pick it up. No contact. Be quick, and do not linger. Return here for further orders."

You don't have any problems along the way. You place the message beneath the flowerpot.

82

TO LEAVE, TURN TO PAGE 88.

TO WAIT AND SEE WHO PICKS UP THE MESSAGE, TURN TO PAGE 90.

"It's best to travel under cover of darkness," Colonel Olney says. "Sleep now, and my aide will wake you at midnight."

You worry about getting lost in the dark, so you stay on the main roads. The sun is rising when you reach General Lafayette's camp. He reads the message quickly.

"Excellent," Lafayette says. "Go eat and sleep. I'll have another mission for you tomorrow."

You are surprised when you hear your next mission. Lafayette asks you to pretend to be loyal to the British.

"Go to Portsmouth, where the British army is camped. They are looking for foragers, men who gather food for the troops and horses," he says. "While you're there, listen to the officers' conversations. When you can, return to me with news of their plans."

TURN THE PAGE.

It's surprisingly easy to get work. The British army is running out of supplies.

During the day, you go to the fields and gather hay for the horses. At night you move through the camp, listening at various campfires. You overhear two officers talking about General Charles Cornwallis, the British commander.

British General
Charles Cornwallis

"We're to go to Yorktown, Virginia, and wait there for the British fleet," one officer says. "Admiral Digby is expected soon. He'll provide the help we need."

You are invisible in the darkness. They continue to talk. "The British navy is the best in the world. We'll win this war," he says.

That night you sneak away. General Lafayette thanks you. Your information helps him plan his attack on the British army.

British soldiers in 1776

TURN TO PAGE 99.

You reach for the message, but the captain grabs it first.

"What have we here?" the captain says, as he looks it over. "It's in code. Gentlemen, I believe we have captured a Patriot spy."

They take you to their camp. The captain gives the message to the major in charge. Your mouth is dry, and your hands are shaking. Spies are hanged.

Patriot Nathan Hale was hanged for spying by the British army on September 22, 1776.

"Where did you get this?" the major asks.

"My master gave it to me," you say. In a way it's true. Before you left, Lafayette said to tell the truth whenever possible. The truth is easier to remember than a lie.

"We'll send the message to Cornwallis to decipher," the major says. "Put the boy to work."

"I can use a slave," the captain says. But the major changes his mind.

"Is your master a Patriot?" the major asks.

"Yes, sir," you say.

"Ah. Then I have a better use for you," he says. "Spy for me, and earn your freedom. But I must warn you. Lie to me, and you die. Get caught by Patriots, and you die. Of course you can say no."

TO SPY FOR THE BRITISH ARMY, TURN TO PAGE 94.

TO REFUSE, TURN TO PAGE 95.

You drop the message as ordered and return to Lafayette's headquarters. A soldier wakes you early the next day.

"General Lafayette says to wear your best clothes," he says. You put on the clothes you wear to serve Mr. Armistead.

"Give me your shoes," Lafayette says. You take them off, and he looks at the heel. "I'll be back."

House slaves often wore silk stockings, breeches, and vests or silk jackets.

While he's gone, Lafayette's aide explains. A cobbler will remove the shoe's heel and hide a message inside. "British General Cornwallis is on his way to Virginia," the aide adds. "We have to get word to the Jersey Brigade."

Your shoes look and feel normal. It's a clever trick. The aide hands you a letter.

"Here is your cover story," the aide says. "If anyone stops you, say you are delivering a message from your master to his sister."

The aide gives you a horse and directions to Williamsburg, Virginia. You are only a few miles from Williamsburg, when you see British soldiers coming in the opposite direction. A side road goes right. It leads to a large farmhouse.

TO CONTINUE ON, TURN TO PAGE 91.

TO TAKE THE SIDE ROAD, TURN TO PAGE 93.

You hide behind a gravestone and wait. It's dark, and you're tired. Soon you're fast asleep. You wake up when someone grabs your shoulder.

"Looks like we've got ourselves a runaway," someone growls.

"I'm not a runaway," you say. "I'm on an errand for my master."

"You're ours now," his partner says.

They tie your hands together and dump you into their wagon. They drive to a British army camp and shove you in front of the major in charge. You repeat your story.

90

The British major rubs his chin. "You have a choice. Stay a slave or join us and earn your freedom. If you agree to gather information we can use, we'll set you free."

TO SPY FOR THE BRITISH ARMY, TURN TO PAGE 94.

TO STAY A SLAVE, TURN TO PAGE 95.

You keep walking. The British army passes by. A few hours later, you find the Jersey Brigade.

"I have a message," you say to the lieutenant.

"Give it to me," he says.

"I can't," you say. "It's in my shoe."

The lieutenant laughs and takes you to his captain. One of the soldiers is a cobbler. He takes the message and repairs your shoe.

"Tell Lafayette that General Rochambeau is a day's march behind us," the captain says.

You begin the journey back to Lafayette. Suddenly three British soldiers surprise you. One nudges you with a musket. You have to think quickly.

91

TO SAY YOU'RE A BRITISH SPY, **TURN TO PAGE 92.**

TO REMAIN SILENT, **TURN TO PAGE 98.**

"What a relief to see you," you say. "I was almost caught by Patriot soldiers."

"Caught?" one soldier asks.

"Caught," you say. "I'm supposed to report to General Cornwallis." It's the name Lafayette's aide mentioned.

"We'll take you to him," the soldiers say.

"General Lafayette is on his way to meet General Washington ...," you tell Cornwallis. Then you remember the Jersey Brigade. " ... in New Jersey."

92

"New Jersey? That changes everything," Cornwallis says. "Go get something to eat. I have another mission for you."

TURN TO PAGE 94.

You turn off before the British soldiers pass. Suddenly men spring from behind the trees. They begin firing at the British soldiers. You turn to see a British officer fall. The British fire back. You are caught between two enemy forces.

A lead ball tears into your back, severing your spinal chord. You die instantly. The fighting ends, and the soldiers move on. No one ever finds the message hidden in your shoe.

skirmish between British soldiers and Patriot militia

THE -END-

To follow another path, turn to page 11.
To read the conclusion, turn to page 101.

You'll become a double agent. You wander around the British army camp and overhear bits of conversation.

"We're moving out in the morning," an officer says. "Cornwallis is going to Yorktown. We'll wait there for ships to carry us north."

It seems like important information. The next morning you report to General Cornwallis' headquarters as ordered.

"I have a message for General Von Bose at Redoubt number 9," General Cornwallis says.

94   It's only a few miles away. Any soldier could carry the message. Perhaps Cornwallis is testing you. You're eager to get the information you've discovered to General Lafayette. Should you go now or wait a few days?

TO RETURN TO LAFAYETTE,
TURN TO PAGE 96.

TO WAIT ANOTHER DAY,
TURN TO PAGE 97.

Spying is dangerous. "I'll stay here," you say.

You do the laundry, cook, fetch water, and feed the captain's horses. You meet other slaves. None of them are free. Before long, red spots appear on your face, hands, and arms.

"You have smallpox," another slave says. She shows you her scars. "I was one of the lucky ones." You aren't. You die of smallpox, still a slave.

*slaves hauling tobacco
in Virginia*

THE
-END-

To follow another path, turn to page 11.
To read the conclusion, turn to page 101.

You must reach General Lafayette. You begin going toward Redoubt number 9 as ordered. But then you circle back. Lafayette's camp is in the opposite direction. You almost reach the outer edge of the camp.

"Halt!" yells a solider.

You run. You're fast, but the soldier is faster. You hear the blast, and then the musket ball hits. Hot, searing pain shoots through your body. You stumble and fall. Blood pours out of your stomach. Seconds later you are dead. You are the first of many to die in Yorktown in September and October 1781.

THE
-END-

To follow another path, turn to page 11.
To read the conclusion, turn to page 101.

Completing this assignment will prove your loyalty to the British. The general at Redoubt number 9 accepts the message.

"No reply," he says, so you return to the British army headquarters.

The next day General Cornwallis and several of his officers leave camp. It's the perfect time to escape. You put your hands in your pockets and walk casually through the camp. As you near the woods, you begin to run.

Four hours later you reach Lafayette. "I was captured by the British," you say.

97

Then you tell Lafayette that Cornwallis is in Yorktown. "He and his troops will wait for the British navy to take them to New York." Lafayette seems pleased.

TURN TO PAGE 99.

You think silence will keep you safe, but it doesn't. The men toss you in the back of a wagon.

Hours later you are tossed aboard a British ship. The ship docks in South Carolina. You're marched to the slave market and sold to a cruel man. You wish you were with Mr. Armistead.

Slaves were sold to the highest bidders at slave markets.

THE
-END-

To follow another path, turn to page 11.
To read the conclusion, turn to page 101.

It isn't long before the Siege of Yorktown begins. General Washington and the French General de Rochambeau arrive to take command. A joint American-French force attacks the British army from land and sea. The armies fight for 22 days before the British surrender. The war is over. America is free.

You are still a slave. William Armistead did not keep his promise. In years to come, you write to the Virginia Legislature and ask for your freedom. After all you are a war hero. It takes six years, but they finally agree to pay Armistead for your freedom. You change your name to Lafayette. At long last you are a free man.

99

To follow another path, turn to page 11.
To read the conclusion, turn to page 101.

British General Cornwallis surrendered to
General Washington at Yorktown on October 19, 1781.

CHAPTER 5

WAR SPIES

At the beginning of the Revolutionary War, the British army had a clear advantage. They were not new to spying. They had years of experience gathering information on their enemies. The Patriots were less prepared to spy on the British army.

Paul Revere and his mechanics were America's first spies. They sent coded messages and signals, and spied on British officers. But they failed to notice that one of Boston's leading Patriots was a British spy. Dr. Benjamin Church attended their meetings and reported what he learned to British General Thomas Gage. Church was arrested as a spy in September 1775 and sent to prison in Boston. In 1778 the Massachusetts Legislature let Church leave for the British island of Martinique. His ship was lost in a storm.

As the war progressed, George Washington became an excellent spymaster. He realized that he would have to create spy networks and pay spies if he wanted the best information. One of his most famous spy rings was the Culper Spy Ring in Long Island. Chapter 2 is based on the experiences of Austin Roe, a Long Island tavern keeper. Roe carried messages for the Culper Spy Ring. He lived to tell his tales.

Revolutionary War spies used many techniques that are still used today. They sent coded letters. They used invisible ink to write between the lines of letters. Some wrote with commonly found ingredients like lemon juice, which disappeared until the paper was heated. Others used chemicals.

Spies wore disguises, stayed in safe houses, and set up dead drops where they left information for other spies. Sometimes spies used hidden compartments to carry messages. For example, a message might be placed inside a musket ball. The spy carried it in a hunting pouch. If caught, he or she could swallow the musket ball.

British army spy Ann Bates used her listening skills, great memory, and ability to go unnoticed to steal secrets. Chapter 3 is based on her adventures. Peddlers, cobblers, women, and teenagers succeeded because they were unexpected spies. That was true of slaves too. James Armistead was a slave who spied for Patriot General Lafayette and eventually earned his freedom. After the war he renamed himself James Lafayette. Chapter 4 is based on his experiences.

103

TURN THE PAGE.

Some spies acted as double agents. They spied for both sides. James Armistead began as a Patriot spy. The British army asked him to spy for them, but he remained a Patriot. Armistead carried misleading messages and battle plans to the British army. It was dangerous to be a double agent.

One of the most well-known double agents in the American Revolution was Continental army General Benedict Arnold. In 1779 he switched sides and began passing information to the British army.

The Culper Spy Ring discovered Arnold was spying for the British army and reported him to George Washington. When Washington tried to arrest him, Arnold escaped. Arnold began fighting for the British army. After the war ended, he moved to England. In America Benedict Arnold is still considered a traitor.

The battles of the American Revolution lasted for eight years. On October 19, 1781, the British surrendered at the Siege of Yorktown in Virginia. The United States became an independent nation. Unlike important generals or heroic soldiers, spies stayed hidden. We know a few by name, but most disappeared into history.

TIMELINE

1765—Secret organizations such as the mechanics form in colonial towns to protest British rule.

1768—British troops arrive in Boston to stop Patriots from rebelling against Great Britain.

1774—The First Continental Congress meets in Philadelphia.

APRIL 19, 1775—The first shots of the war are fired at Lexington and Concord, Massachusetts.

JUNE 15, 1775—Continental Congress names George Washington commander in chief of the Continental army.

JULY 4, 1776—Congress ratifies the Declaration of Independence.

SEPT. 19, 1777—Philadelphia falls to the British army.

FEB. 6, 1778—France joins the Revolutionary War on the side of the Patriots.

JUNE 18, 1778—The British army leaves Philadelphia.

AUG. 1778—British army spy Ann Bates goes to White Plains, New York, to learn General Washington's plans.

1778—George Washington creates the Culper Spy Ring under Benjamin Tallmadge.

1779—Patriot General Benedict Arnold switches sides and becomes a British army spy.

OCT. 1781—British General Cornwallis surrenders in Yorktown, Virginia. It is the last major battle in the war.

SEPT. 1783—Leaders from the United States and Great Britain sign the Treaty of Paris.

OCTOBER–NOVEMBER 1783—British troops leave America.

MAY 25, 1787—The Constitutional Convention begins in Philadelphia.

1789—George Washington becomes the first president of the United States.

OTHER PATHS TO EXPLORE

In this book you've seen what it was like to be a spy during the Revolutionary War. Perspectives in history are as varied as the people who lived it. Seeing history from many points of view is an important part of understanding it.

Here are some ideas for other points of view to explore:

+ Both the Patriots and British army used secret codes. One of the simplest was a substitution code. One letter takes the place of another letter in the alphabet. Some used numbers instead of letters. Imagine General Washington asks you to develop a substitution code. What would that code look like? (Integration of Knowledge and Ideas)

+ Spies had to be careful observers. So did those who caught spies. What would it be like to suspect a neighbor of spying? What steps would you take to prove the person's guilt or innocence? (Integration of Knowledge and Ideas)

+ During the American Revolution, French soldiers fought with the Patriots. German soldiers, called Hessians, fought for the British army. What role do you think language played in the war? How do you think this would affect a spy's work? (Integration of Knowledge and Ideas)

READ MORE

Bearce, Stephanie. *The American Revolution.* Top Secret Files. **Waco, Texas: Prufrock Press, Inc., 2015.**

Hale, Nathan. *One Dead Spy: The Life, Times, and Last Words of Nathan Hale, America's Most Famous Spy.* **Nathan Hale's Hazardous Tales. New York: Amulet Books, 2012.**

Micklos, Jr., John. *Why We Won the American Revolution— Through Primary Sources.* **The American Revolution Through Primary Sources. Berkeley Heights, N.J.: Enslow Publishers, 2013.**

Raum, Elizabeth. *A Revolutionary War Timeline.* **Smithsonian War Timelines. North Mankato, Minn.: Capstone Press, 2014.**

INTERNET SITES

Use FactHound to find Internet sites related to this book. All of the sites on FactHound have been researched by our staff.

Here's all you do:
Visit *www.facthound.com*
Type in this code: 9781491458587

GLOSSARY

bayonet (BAY-uh-net)—a long knife that can be fastened to the end of a rifle

brigade (bri-GAYD)—a unit of an army

commander (kuh-MAND-ur)—someone who has control over a group of people in the military

cove (KOVE)—a small, sheltered bay near the shores of a sea, river, or lake

decipher (di-SYE-fur)—to figure out something that is written in code or hard to understand

disguise (diss-GIZE)—to dress in a way that hides who you really are

master (MASS-tur)—a person who owns slaves

militia (muh-LISH-uh)—citizens who serve as soldiers

110 **musket** (MUHSS-kit)—a gun with a long barrel

ratify (RAT-uh-fye)—to agree to or approve officially

redoubt (ri-DOUT)—a small fort made of dirt

regiment (REJ-uh-muhnt)—a large group of soldiers who fight together

sentry (SEN-tree)—a person who stands guard

token (TOH-kuhn)—item that stands for something else

BIBLIOGRAPHY

Allen, Thomas B. *Tories: Fighting for the King in America's First Civil War.* New York: Harper, 2010.

Bellesiles, Michael. *James Armistead Lafayette.* Encyclopedia of the American Revolution: Library of Military History. Ed. Harold E. Selesky. Detroit: Charles Scribner's Sons, 2006.

Crews, Ed. *Spies and Scouts, Secret Writing, and Sympathetic Citizens.* Colonial Williamsburg. CWJournal: Summer 04, 2004. http://www.history.org/Foundation/journal/Summer04/spies.cfm.

Hambucken, Denis and Bill Payson. *Soldier of the American Revolution: A Visual Reference.* Woodstock, Vt.: Countryman Press, 2011.

Kilmeade, Brian and Don Yaeger. *George Washington's Secret Six: The Spy Ring that Saved the American Revolution.* New York: Sentinel, 2013.

Nagy, John A. *Invisible Ink: Spycraft of the American Revolution.* Yardley, Penn.: Westholme, 2011.

Sulik, Michael J. *Spying in America: Espionage from the Revolutionary War to the Dawn of the Cold War.* Washington, D.C.: Georgetown U. P., 2012.

Williams, Victoria. *"Culper Spy Ring."* George Washington's Mount Vernon. N.p., n.d. Web. http://www.mountvernon.org/educational-resources/encyclopedia/culper-spy-ring.

INDEX